MEDITATION
for beginners

by Wild Pebble

Meditation for Beginners

Welcome To Your Meditation Guide & Journal

Congratulations! You have just taken the first wonderful step to developing your own personal meditation practice. You may have come to meditation out of curiosity or through recommendation, either way you are about to embark on a journey of discovery that can help you gain a deeper sense of calm inner peace.

Through a series of simple steps this book will help you to begin and develop a positive meditation practice so that it becomes a natural part of your life. It will be your guide, companion, and journal.

For more experienced meditators this book can help reinvigorate your meditations and enhance your personal approach to meditation.

Meditation has a long history and many different traditions that have guided and influenced its development over many years. This range and variety in meditation styles can be seen as a positive, it offers choice. Yet also confusing, where to begin?

This is where this Guide and Journal comes in. It can be seen as a starting point for you to learn, develop and grow.

This guide and journal will:

- Be your gentle introduction to meditation.

- Support you to learn at your own pace.

- Encourage you to develop your motivation and commitment so that meditation becomes a natural part of your life.

- Help you to reflect on your meditation and celebrate your achievements.

The beauty of this practice is that, as you progress, you can choose to explore different styles and adopt a method that fits with you. This is important. You have choice and freedom to find what works for you. In the here and now, the style of meditation that works is the one that works best for YOU.

This Guide and Journal is not set out to be a comprehensive guide to types and styles of meditation, rather it is here to help you to begin your journey into meditation through a series of gentle steps so that you feel gently guided and supported along the way. Imagine this book as your guide and companion on a journey.

How to use your Guide & Journal

To help you with your meditation journey this book is set out in two parts. Part 1 will be your Guide and Part 2, your Journal. Let's look at these now.

Part 1: Your Guide

The Guide will help you to:

- Look at why people meditate, perceptions of meditation and to become more aware of the benefits of meditation.

- Get started with meditating through a series of gentle steps. With each step there are short exercises that aim to support you to learn and develop a personal approach to meditation. The focus here is to develop a Calm Breath, Calm Body, and Calm Mind.

- Develop your own motivation and commitment to meditation. This will help you to allow meditation to be a natural part of your life and an every-day habit. By taking a gentle approach you can build your motivation and commitment over time. The Guide will help you to look at your motivation and how you can approach your commitment.

Part 2: Your Journal

The Journal provides:

- An overview and gentle guidance to a series of short meditation sessions. These are set out to help you build an ongoing meditation practice.

- Space for you to note comments and personal reflections, and a weekly 'check in' point to help you reflect on progress.

- You with the ability to track your meditation habit and to be aware of challenges and progress.

By working with the Journal, you can develop your meditation habit. Also, the beauty of Journalling is it helps you to reflect on your experiences, challenges, and progress. This helps you to be open and to see what is working and what you can work on. The journal can help strengthen your motivation and commitment. Remember, this is time for you and by keeping a journal you can value your experiences and celebrate your achievements.

PART 1
YOUR GUIDE

Simple Steps For
CALM
INNER PEACE

PART 1: YOUR GUIDE

Chapter 1: Open To All

Why do people choose meditation?

Meditation comes into people's lives for many different reasons. Examples here include:

- Life's Challenges: They may be feeling stressed, have a lack of sleep, going through an emotional crisis, work pressures, or feeling unhappy with their current situation.

- Recommendation: Meditation was recommended by a friend, doctor or therapist who felt that meditation could help them.

- Personal Development: They felt that meditation would help them with a personal interest or belief.

- Curiosity: They read or heard an article on meditation that they felt a need to explore this further.

These are all examples that help us to see that people, of all ages and backgrounds, come to meditation for different reasons. This also helps us to see that meditation is open to all.

We can acknowledge the challenges that many people have in their lives. A busy lifestyle, numerous commitments, a life crisis, distractions, different stresses, and concerns. Over time these can accumulate and affect us physically, emotionally, and psychologically. Meditation is something that many people make a conscious choice to explore.

Perceptions of meditation

For some people their perception of meditation affects their motivation or commitment to taking up meditation. For example, people may:

- Feel they cannot do meditation, it's too hard or complicated.
- Think I'm not that type of person, it's for hippies.
- Say "I don't have the patience".
- Feel their mind is too busy.
- Say they don't have the time.

Let's think about these for a moment.

1. Let's pause and take the view that sometimes it's good to try something before dismissing it totally. We can take a gentle leap into trying something first hand.

2. People from all walks of life have an ongoing motivation and commitment to meditation. It is not 'just for hippies'. It is open to all.

3. We can allow time for ourselves, even two or five minutes a day to meditate is a start point. Yes, we can be busy, yet in those 24-hour days of our lives we have the capacity to choose time for ourselves, to be calm and feel inner peace.

4. We can release ourselves from old habits and perceptions and look forward to a future where we can feel motivated and committed to the benefits of meditation. In many ways this is self-care. By gaining a deeper understanding of the benefits of meditation we can start to develop a more open and positive view.

Many of life's experiences come from trying something first hand. This is one of the main ways we all learn, we try it out, we find out how it 'fits' with us. Sometimes we learn things quickly, and other times it takes longer. Also, learning can be seen as part of the journey of our lives. Sometimes in life we are too focused on the destination (the end 'product') that we may miss out on the joy and wonder of the journey (the experience and the learning itself).

By being more aware of the benefits of meditation we can improve our perception of meditation and allow ourselves to feel more motivated and positive about meditation.

The Benefits of Meditation

There are many positive reasons for why we should meditate. Examples of the benefits to meditating include:

Health and Wellbeing:
There are a range of studies that have shown that meditation can help to reduce stress levels, alleviate anxiety, and help with sleeplessness. By feeling calm your mind and body can become less stressed. Meditation can also help you with developing a healthier lifestyle.

Personal Development:
The process of meditation helps you to develop a deeper understanding of yourself. You develop the ability to be in the moment, to feel calm in the moment. You are not worrying about the past or the future. You can begin to take a broader view on life and worry less about meaningless things.

Relationships:
As your meditation practice develops you can build a greater sense of compassion and loving kindness. This can help you to have more meaningful and positive relationships.

Spiritual Development
For some people meditation can be a part of their spiritual development, to gain a better understanding of their life's purpose.

The spiritual aspect may not be a focus for everyone. With that in mind the Guide is set out in a non-spiritual way to allow choice in your focus and outcomes you seek.

Your approach and your beliefs can help underpin your own style of meditation. It can be a spiritual approach or not. The key thing here is that meditation is personal to you, it is your choice.

Meditation: The Ripple Effect

When looking at the benefits of meditation it is possible to see how meditation has the potential to have a positive ripple effect to ourselves and our lives.

For example:

- When we feel calm, we can be more open to handling challenging situations and stress in our life.

- Meditation can help you to be more compassionate. By being more compassionate and open we can build healthy relationships.

- Meditation can help you feel more connected to the moments in your life, in this way you can value the here and now.

- By meditating in a nature setting, you can experience the wonder of nature in a totally different way. This can help you feel more aware of your relationship with nature.

Meditation can help us to experience calm and inner peace that can move us towards developing more healthy habits. We can be more open and compassionate. We can take care of ourselves in a way that allows us to take a wider perspective to life's challenges. We can value the here and now. Where moments in life matter.

The next Chapter will help you begin to develop your own meditation practice, starting with some simple steps to help you along the way.

Chapter 2: Calm Breath, Body, and Mind

Sometimes in life when we keep things simple, we can achieve more. The approach in this guide is to allow meditation to be based on three simple memorable steps. This helps your mind to have a clear gentle focus. These steps are:

1. Calm Breath
2. Calm Body
3. Calm Mind

This Chapter will guide you on each step and help you to practice each one.

Before looking at these three steps you will need to have a place to meditate and a posture to help you meditate comfortably.

Let's look at these now.

Location & Posture

Location:

Before you begin meditating it helps to have a location to meditate that will work for you. Many people find that their home is a safe place to do their meditation practice. The key thing is to have a place that you can feel comfortable in and not be disturbed.

You may also find a location outdoors where you are in nature. Ideally a setting where you can feel comfortable and safe. This could be in a park, by a river, a forest, or in the mountains. Nature is a lovely place to meditate and can add something special to your meditation.

It also helps to have a location that, by developing a habit of meditation, can be associated with meditation. It is your 'go to' safe place.

Posture:

For each meditation you will find it helps to have a posture that is relaxed yet 'alert'. This may sound odd saying 'relaxed yet alert', yet you can do this where your body is in a relaxed state and your posture is alert, 'awake'.

You may wish to sit cross legged on the floor or upright on a chair. The key thing here is to be in a position that allows your back to be upright and supported.

Your hands can be resting on your lap or on the edge of your knees. Palms facing up can feel energising, palms facing down can feel more grounding.

Aim to find a posture you feel comfortable with and a location that allows you space to meditate – this is your safe space.

Allow yourself to have no expectations. This is your time to learn and grow. Let's begin with Calm Breath.

Step 1: Calm the Breath

Meditation begins with the breath. It is your main guide and pathway into your body and mind. It is a powerful life force that connects to you and helps to calm the body and mind.

We very rarely sit quietly and focus on our breath so at first your breath may feel slightly tense, this is normal, you are taking your first steps to calming your breath. Ease into this slowly, relax and allow your focus to be gentle and calm, slow down and take this time to feel calm in your breath.

When you experience calm breathing, this sends a message to your body and mind that all is well, you are safe.

To help you with this let's try a couple of short exercises. The aim in these exercises is to be aware of your Calm Breath, to feel connected to your breath, to be aware of how your breath can help you feel calm.

For each of the exercises that follow read the guidance first then carry out the exercise.

Exercise 1: Breath in Numbers

Guidance:

- Find your safe location.

- Find your comfortable posture - relaxed yet alert.

- Close your eyes.

- Breathe in through your nose slowly - count 1 to 4, then pause, then breathe out slowly - count 1 to 4, pause.

- Now repeat – In for 4, pause, out for 4, pause.

- Focus on the breath – feel the breath going in... and ... out.

- Do this gently and be aware of your breath feeling calm.

Try this for two minutes.

Once you finish, allow yourself to come back into your space. Open your eyes. Stay still for a moment and feel the calm in you.

Exercise 2: Belly Breathing

This exercise is aimed at helping to you to be more aware of your breath and your body.

Guidance:

- Find your safe location and comfortable posture.

- Place one hand gently on your stomach, close your eyes.

- As you breath in allow your belly to move out, feel this movement in your hand.

- As you breath out allow your belly to gently move back in.

- In this exercise there is less movement of your chest while breathing. Practice this calmly and slowly. Feel the rise and fall of your belly.

- Feel your belly moving out as you breathe in.

- Feel your belly moving in as you breathe out.

After a few times of this breath take your hand away and carry on this approach to Belly Breath. Stay calm and focused on the movement of your belly. Try this for two minutes.

Once you finish, allow yourself to come back into your space. Open your eyes. Stay still for a moment and feel the calm in you.

Allow yourself to also try this exercise during the day. By doing this you are building 'muscle memory' into the rhythm of your breathing. Eventually this will become a pattern of breathing that becomes second nature and natural.

Step 2: Calm the Body

The aim of this next exercise is to be aware of your body, to notice areas of tension and to gently release that tension so that you feel calm, safe, and grounded.

To help you do this you will carry out a Body Scan. This approach allows you to gently focus on your body and to soften areas of tension.

By doing this exercise:

- Your body has a calm and peaceful feeling.
- You will feel alert, yet relaxed.
- You will feel grounded and connected to yourself.

Exercise 3 : Calm Body

This will be your 'Calm the Body' session where you can allow yourself some 'me' time.

The Body Scan is a way for you to focus on parts of your body, to pay attention to that area, to allow that area to relax and soften. It is a gentle process. Be present in the moment and allow yourself to feel your body slowly calming, whilst remaining alert.

Guidance:

- Find your safe location and comfortable posture.

- Close your eyes, allow your Calm Breath to be present.

- Notice how your body feels.

- Now begin your Body Scan. Start at the top.

- Bring your focus to your forehead, then eyes, then cheeks, and then jaw.

- Silently use words to yourself to help Calm these areas.

- 'Soften' 'Relax' 'Calm'. For example - Soften Eyes, Relax Forehead.   (continued on next page)

- Move down - Calm Shoulders, soften arms and hands.

- Stay here in this moment now. Feel the Calmness of your body.

- Move down to your chest, stomach, and legs.

- Remember, your aim is to be calm and alert. Keep your back and spine gently straight so that you feel supported and relaxed. You feel alert and aware.

Try this for two minutes.

Once you finish, allow yourself to come back into your space. Open your eyes. Stay still for a moment and feel the calm in you.

How do you feel? Think of two of three short words that describe this. You may feel lighter, more relaxed. Allow this feeling of calmness to stay with you.

Step 3: Calm the Mind

Having a Calm Breath and Calm Body will help you to set the foundations for a Calm Mind. Bringing these all together will help you begin your meditation journey.

To help you move towards your Calm Mind the following guidance will help you.

When you begin you will become aware of thoughts. Allow yourself to acknowledge them and let them pass and come back to the area of focus. For this exercise your breath is the focus.

Each time you have a thought recognise it, then come back to your breath. Allow yourself to feel calm and centred.

Allow yourself to have no expectations.

Free yourself from concerns, this is your time.

Exercise 4: Calm Mind

Guidance:

- Find your safe location and comfortable posture.

- Close your eyes, feel your Calm Breath. You feel safe.

- Release tensions to feel your Calm Body.

- Now focus on your breath.

- Breathe gently in and out.

- As thoughts arise allow them to pass. Come back to your breath. Allow yourself to have a gentle focus on your breath. (continued on next page)

- You are allowing yourself to have a Calm Mind.

- Each time a thought arises, allow it to pass, come back to your breath.

Try this for three minutes.

When finished, allow yourself time to gently come back from your meditation. Spend a moment to feel Calm in your breath, body, and mind. Carry this feeling into your day.

Exercise 4 is the foundation to your meditation journey and one that you will return to in Part 2, your Journal.

Summary

As a gentle reminder of your journey so far:

Location
You have found a location that works for you. It is your safe 'go to' place for meditating.

Posture
You have started to develop a posture that helps you to meditate where your body is relaxed yet alert.

Calm Breath

You are more aware of your breath and how it can help you feel relaxed, grounded and calm.

Calm Body

You can now scan your body and help it to relax, while remaining alert in your posture.

Calm Mind

You have started to join your Calm Breath and Calm Body with your Calm Mind. You can recognise thoughts, allow them to pass, and use your breath as a focus in your meditation.

Before we move on to Part 2, your Journal, it will help to look at:

1. Three key areas that can influence your meditation practice and how you can approach them. These are your thoughts, distractions, and emotions.

2. Understanding your motivation and commitment to meditation. These are here because without these developing a meditation habit is less likely to succeed. Your motivation and commitment can help you to allow meditation to be a natural part of your daily life.

Chapter 3: Thoughts, Distractions & Emotions

Thoughts

Thoughts are natural.

Yet in meditation they are one of the key challenges to your meditation practice. By taking a gentle approach you can be more open to your thoughts as being natural. You can adopt different approaches so that thoughts become less intrusive to your calm inner peace.

Try one of the following approaches when thoughts arise:

1. Recognise your thoughts as they arise and let them go. Come back to your breath (or the area of focus you are using).

2. Allow the thought to happen. Then come back to your breath (or your area of focus you are using).

3. Name the thought. This could be 'planning, planning'... 'remembering, remembering'...'thinking, thinking'... and let it pass. Come back to your breath. Each time a thought arises gently name it, then let it go, come back to your focus.

With thoughts, aim to make no judgement, stay neutral. Allow them to pass.

Distractions

Distractions may come in the form of physical sensations.

With physical sensations try naming them. For example, 'tingling, tingling', 'tense, tense' or whatever you sense the feeling is. Aim to ease into the physical sensations, and where possible relax that area, focus on it, and allow it to feel calm. Come back to your calm breath.

Emotions

During a meditation session you may experience different emotions.

Allow yourself to take a non-judgemental approach to your emotions. Where possible seek to be an observer and allow them to pass. Come back to your focus, your calm breath.

For some people the emotions may be more intense during meditation, such as crying or feeling upset. This can be seen as a form of release. Take time out to relax and focus on your breath. Allow yourself to breath calmly, to feel calm and feel grounded.

Experiencing different emotions during meditation is common. If you have intense emotions during meditation you may wish to talk about them with a trusted friend or seek the support of a counselor or therapist.

Chapter 4: Motivation and Commitment

When we seek to start a new habit, it helps to pause and reflect on two key areas that can help the habit become a natural part of our lives. These can be seen as Motivation and Commitment. They are the springboards to moving forward. Let's look at these now.

Motivation – Your Future Self

Your future self can be influenced by your intentions now. You are motivating yourself now to help your future self. You are building an emotional connection to your future identity and where you want to be. You are also motivating yourself towards the benefits of mediation and how they will help your future self.

Try this mini exercise to build that emotional connection. Read the guidance first then carry out the mini exercise.

Exercise 5: Motivation

Guidance:

- Find your safe location and comfortable posture.
- Close your eyes, feel your Calm Breath. You feel safe.
- Now imagine your future self. See and feel yourself meditating.

- Now say to yourself:

  I am in my safe space.
  I am calm.
  I feel rested and at ease.
  I feel compassionate and more open.

Stay with this focus on seeing and feeling your future self for two or three minutes. This can help you to build an emotional connection to your future self and help build your motivation.

After this mini exercise complete this next section. It will help you strengthen your motivation.

To help you focus your motivation look back at pages 14-16 on the benefits of meditation. This will help you have a clear focus on the benefits you are working towards, those that motivate you.

My Motivation

Meditation will help my future self in the following ways:

1.

2.

3.

Commitment – Habits Matter

In life you could have one, two or three strategies to achieve a goal or an outcome. Yet without commitment they will not work. Commitment can be seen in many ways. One approach to developing commitment is to keep it simple and small so that it becomes a habit, it becomes a natural part of your daily life.

With meditation you can aim to start small. Allow yourself two minutes to meditate. Commit to once a day at a certain time of day.

You can also fit in mini meditations during your day. Even to pause and adopt a Calm Breath, to slow down briefly is a beginning. Be kind to yourself in the day.

By developing a habit, you are building commitment. Over time you can gently extend your meditation time from two to five minutes. The choice is yours. You move forward at your own pace.

We all have some level of daily routine, our habits. Things we do on a regular basis. We have habits that are not necessarily named as habits as they are second nature in your daily life – cleaning your teeth, cooking a meal, taking a shower, getting dressed, everyday normal things.

Look at your habits and identify a time when you can allow yourself 2 or 5 minutes to have a short gentle meditation session.

For some people the morning is an ideal time as you are fresh to the day. The meditation can help you feel calm, at ease, more open. You can take this feeling into your day.

Imagine how lovely that would be! To start your day with a calm positive mindset.

You may also feel that meditation works better for you in the evening when the day has ended. This can help you relax and reduce the stresses of the day. Perhaps after your evening meal or before you go to sleep.

The key thing here is to find a time of day where you can add meditation alongside existing habits. This helps it to become a natural part of your day.

For this next part you can set out a series of short statements where you set out in clear terms how you will commit to developing a meditation habit. Aim to be specific. For example:

I will:
- Find a location that will be my meditation space.
- Meditate once a day in the morning for two minutes.
- Complete my reflection journal after each session.

Now it's your turn. Set out your commitment below.

My Commitment

To develop meditation as an ongoing natural habit I will:

1.

2.

3.

Meditation In Your Life

Congratulations! You have now taken the first steps to feeling motivated and building your commitment to meditation.

By taking small steps you are allowing this to be time for you. You can remove the pressure of feeling it is 'taking time' – as it is becoming a habit. Also, in many ways, meditation is 'giving time'. How? Well, meditation gives you time to pause, to be calm, to feel connected to yourself. Remember, meditation has many benefits that you are giving to yourself.

This guide and journal aims to help you to see meditation as a normal, healthy add-on to your habits. You can do this.

Learning to meditate is an experience and a journey. As you meditate allow yourself to release any expectations and to focus on being in the moment of your meditation.

For some people there can be a sense of frustration or concern about not 'doing it right'. Yet you will, over time, become more in tune with your meditation. Remember, this is a journey and not a race. Allow your experience of meditation to gently grow over time. By using a journal you will be able to see your progress.

Let's go forward to Part 2, your Journal. Here you can set your own pace and build commitment and confidence over time.

The Journal provides gentle guidance and space for you to reflect on your meditation journey. The Journal is also your Companion, it aims to support and inspire you.

PART 2
YOUR JOURNAL

Simple Steps For

CALM

INNER PEACE

PART 2: YOUR JOURNAL

Your Journal is your safe place to reflect on your meditation practice. It is set out in a way that aims to keep your meditations gentle and accessible. Along the way the Journal provides support and inspiration to help you in the form of your Companion.

With the meditation sessions that follow aim to start small and to keep your sessions regular. Over time gently build your time spent meditating. For example, aim for two to five minutes in your early sessions then move onto ten minutes. A key item to note here is that it is not about how long you meditate, it is more about the quality of your meditation.

You may find that over time it becomes natural and comfortable to allow ten minutes of quality meditation to be a natural part of your day.

After each meditation exercise it will help you to fill out the reflection page. This helps you to capture your session, what worked and any challenges you experienced. It can also help you to see and feel your own development.

Companion Message:

Remember, you are building a positive habit that will benefit you now and into the future. Allow yourself to celebrate your achievements as you continue your meditation journey.

Let's begin with a meditation that will help you to have a calm focus. This will help you continue to develop your approach to having a Calm Breath, Body, and Mind.

Remember to read the guidance first, then carry out the meditation session.

Chapter 5: Pure Calm Meditation

Guidance:

- Find your safe location and comfortable posture.

- Close your eyes and allow yourself to feel your Calm Breath.

- Calm your Body, release any tension.

- Use the following words as your focus:

    - As you breathe in silently say to yourself 'Pure'
    - As you breathe out say to yourself 'Calm'.
      This helps to calm the body and mind.

- As thoughts arise allow them to pass. Come back to your focus – 'Pure' 'Calm'. Allow yourself to have a gentle focus on these words.

- You are allowing yourself to have a Calm Mind

- Each time a thought arises, allow it to pass, come back to the words, 'Pure' 'Calm'.

Try this for three minutes.

When you finish, allow yourself time to gently come back from your meditation. Spend a moment to feel Calm in your breath, body, and mind. Carry this feeling into your day.

Aim to carry out this meditation over the next seven days.

The Journal now has seven pages for you to reflect on these sessions. The seventh session includes a weekly review. This review is aimed at helping you to look back over your sessions.

Reflection Page (1)

Date: Location:

Guidance: Use short sentences or two or three words for each item. This will help you focus on the items that stand out. Keep it simple.

From this Meditation:

- Describe how you felt during and after this session:

- Describe any challenges you experienced during the session (thoughts, emotions, physical sensations):

- As a result of this session describe any benefits you can see from this session:

Reflection Page (2)

Date: Location:

Guidance: Use short sentences or two or three words for each item. This will help you focus on the items that stand out. Keep it simple.

From this Meditation:

- Describe how you felt during and after this session:

- Describe any challenges you experienced during the session (thoughts, emotions, physical sensations):

- As a result of this session describe any benefits you can see from this session:

Reflection Page (3)

Date: Location:

Guidance: Use short sentences or two or three words for each item. This will help you focus on the items that stand out. Keep it simple.

From this Meditation:

- Describe how you felt during and after this session:

- Describe any challenges you experienced during the session (thoughts, emotions, physical sensations):

- As a result of this session describe any benefits you can see from this session:

Reflection Page (4)

Date: Location:

Guidance: Use short sentences or two or three words for each item. This will help you focus on the items that stand out. Keep it simple.

From this Meditation:

- Describe how you felt during and after this session:

- Describe any challenges you experienced during the session (thoughts, emotions, physical sensations):

- As a result of this session describe any benefits you can see from this session:

Reflection Page (5)

Date: Location:

Guidance: Use short sentences or two or three words for each item. This will help you focus on the items that stand out. Keep it simple.

From this Meditation:

- Describe how you felt during and after this session:

- Describe any challenges you experienced during the session (thoughts, emotions, physical sensations):

- As a result of this session describe any benefits you can see from this session:

Reflection Page (6)

Date: Location:

Guidance: Use short sentences or two or three words for each item. This will help you focus on the items that stand out. Keep it simple.

From this Meditation:

- Describe how you felt during and after this session:

- Describe any challenges you experienced during the session (thoughts, emotions, physical sensations):

- As a result of this session describe any benefits you can see from this session:

Reflection Page (7) and Weekly Review

Date: Location:

Thinking about today and your previous sessions this week, reflect on your meditations.

Today's Session:

Weekly Review – Looking Back

- Summarize your overall experience of your meditations:

- Describe any recurring challenges and how you approached them:

- Describe how your meditations have helped you:

- What are you proud of this week? Allow yourself to celebrate successes and achievements:

Companion Message:

Congratulations! You have now completed seven sessions of meditation. You have started to allow meditation to be a natural part of your day.

Let's keep going!

Chapter 6: Meditation Development

This Chapter will help you to move forward and develop your meditation practice.

You will now have an opportunity to try out seven different approaches to meditation. This will help add variety to your practice.

This can help with motivation and commitment by helping you:

- to grow your practice
- to keep momentum in your commitment
- to develop wider experiences of meditation

Each meditation will provide you with guidance and then a reflection page. Remember, by completing your journal and reflecting on your meditation you can see and feel how this is helping you. After these seven meditations there is a weekly review page to help you reflect on your meditation journey so far.

For each meditation read the guidance first, then gently follow the guidance.

Belly Breath Meditation

Guidance:

- Find your safe location and comfortable posture.

- Close your eyes and allow yourself to feel your Calm Breath.

- Calm your Body, release any tension.

- Place one hand gently on your stomach.

- As you breathe in allow your belly to move out, feel this movement in your hand.

- As you breathe out allow your belly to gently move back in.

- Feel your belly moving out as you breathe in.

- Feel your belly moving in as you breathe out.

- As thoughts arise allow them to pass. Come back to your belly breath. Allow yourself to have a gentle focus on your belly breath. Feel your Calm Mind

- Each time a thought arises, allow it to pass, come back to your breath.
(continued on next page)

After a few times of this breath take your hand away and carry on this approach to Belly Breath. Stay calm and focussed on the movement of your belly. Your gentle calm breath moving in and out.

Try this for three minutes. When you finish stay still for a while and feel Calm Inner Peace.

Reflection Page (8)

Date: Location:

Guidance: Use short sentences or two or three words for each item. This will help you focus on the items that stand out. Keep it simple.

From this Meditation:

- Describe how you felt during and after this session:

- Describe any challenges you experienced during the session (thoughts, emotions, physical sensations):

- As a result of this session describe any benefits you can see from this session:

Breath in Numbers Meditation

Guidance:

- Find your safe location and comfortable posture

- Close your eyes.

- Breathe in through your nose - count 1 to 4, then pause, then breathe out slowly - count 1 to 4, pause.

- Now repeat – Inhale for 4 seconds, pause, exhale for 4 seconds, pause.

- Focus on the breath – feel the breath going in... and ... out.

- Do this gently and be aware of your breath feeling calm.

- As thoughts arise allow them to pass. Come back to your breath, gently counting your breath going in and out.

- You are allowing yourself to have a Calm Mind. Each time a thought arises, allow it to pass, come back to your breath.

Try this for three minutes. When you finish stay still for a while and feel Calm Inner Peace.

Reflection Page (9)

Date: Location:

Guidance: Use short sentences or two or three words for each item. This will help you focus on the items that stand out. Keep it simple.

From this Meditation:

- Describe how you felt during and after this session:

- Describe any challenges you experienced during the session (thoughts, emotions, physical sensations):

- As a result of this session describe any benefits you can see from this session:

Loving Kindness Meditation: To Yourself

In this meditation the focus is on sending loving kindness to yourself using positive phrases.

Guidance:

- Find your safe location and comfortable posture.

- Close your eyes and allow yourself to feel your Calm Breath.

- Calm your Body, release any tension.

- Silently repeat to yourself two or three positive, reassuring phrases. The messages below are examples, but you can also create your own:
  May I be happy and safe.
  May I be well in body and mind.
  May I be calm and at peace.

- As thoughts arise allow them to pass. Come back to your focus, your phrases. Allow yourself to have a gentle focus on these words.

- You are allowing yourself to have a Calm Mind

Try this for three minutes. When you finish, stay still for a while, and feel Calm Inner Peace.

Reflection Page (10)

Date: Location:

Guidance: Use short sentences or two or three words for each item. This will help you focus on the items that stand out. Keep it simple.

From this Meditation:

- Describe how you felt during and after this session:

- Describe any challenges you experienced during the session (thoughts, emotions, physical sensations):

- As a result of this session describe any benefits you can see from this session:

Defrost Meditation

This meditation is one that you can try out during the day. It can be seen as a mini meditation. Here the aim is to be aware of the body, of areas of tension. To relax and to 'defrost' areas of tension.

Guidance:

- Find your safe location and comfortable posture.

- Close your eyes and allow yourself to feel your Calm Breath.

- Calm your Body, release any tension.

- With your breath as a focus, on each out-breath release tension, feel soft.

- Silently say to yourself 'soft' on the out breath, releasing tension across your body.

- Feel your body relaxing, feel calm and soft.

- Feel your breath, body and mind becoming calm on each out breath.

Try this for three minutes. When you finish stay still for a while and feel Calm Inner Peace.

Reflection Page (11)

Date: Location:

Guidance: Use short sentences or two or three words for each item. This will help you focus on the items that stand out. Keep it simple.

From this Meditation:

- Describe how you felt during and after this session:

- Describe any challenges you experienced during the session (thoughts, emotions, physical sensations):

- As a result of this session describe any benefits you can see from this session:

Loving Kindness Meditation: To Others

This meditation helps to add a 'loving' element where you are sending loving kindness to others. This could be a person, a group of people or even a cause you wish to help.

In this meditation aim to visualise your intention to send loving kindness. You can imagine that the person or the cause you have in mind is surrounded and filled with a color that can be associated with positivity, for example:

- A soft green for healing.

- Pink for love and kindness.

- A calm white for purity.

Before you begin – decide who it is for and have a color in mind.

Guidance:

- Find your safe location and comfortable posture.

- Close your eyes and allow yourself to feel your Calm Breath.

- Calm your Body, release any tension.

- Visualise the person, group, or cause.

- Imagine them being gently surrounded with the color you have in mind. Keep that feeling of sending the color and the color being present.

- Feel loving kindness being sent.

- Stay here, in this moment, visualise the color staying.

Try this for three minutes. When you finish stay still for a while and feel Calm Inner Peace.

Reflection Page (12)

Date: Location:

Guidance: Use short sentences or two or three words for each item. This will help you focus on the items that stand out. Keep it simple.

From this Meditation:

- Describe how you felt during and after this session:

- Describe any challenges you experienced during the session (thoughts, emotions, physical sensations):

- As a result of this session describe any benefits you can see from this session:

Nature Meditation

Meditating in the outdoors can help add variety to your practice and help you feel more connected to your environment and the planet. It is a special form of meditation. Find a safe location outdoors where you can be with nature. This could be your local park, your back garden, a forest, by a stream.

Guidance:

- Settle into your safe location.

- Close your eyes.

- Find your Calm Breath and Calm Body.

- Notice the sounds around you, feel the wind on your skin, be aware of nature around you.

- Allow yourself to feel connected to the nature around you.

- When thoughts arise come back to nature. Listen, feel, and sense nature around you.

- Stay still and calm, breathe and feel connected to nature.

Try this for three minutes. When you finish stay still for a while and feel Calm Inner Peace.

Reflection Page (13)

Date: Location:

Guidance: Use short sentences or two or three words for each item. This will help you focus on the items that stand out. Keep it simple.

From this Meditation:

- Describe how you felt during and after this session:

- Describe any challenges you experienced during the session (thoughts, emotions, physical sensations):

- As a result of this session describe any benefits you can see from this session:

In the Moment Meditation

This meditation is less about areas of focus that support your practice. The breath can be your initial focus yet, in this meditation, you are becoming more aware and present of being in the moment. Start with a focus on the breath and then gently release yourself from this focus. Feel more in the moment. Be aware of yourself in the here and now. Allow yourself to just be.

Guidance:

- Find your safe location and comfortable posture.

- Close your eyes and feel your Calm Breath.

- Calm your Body, release any tension.

- Be aware of your breath, moving in and out.

- Gently allow your focus to move to the 'moment'.

- You feel still and calm. Gently let thoughts pass.

- Become calm inner peace.
  (continued on next page)

- Thoughts may appear, let them pass.

- Stay here for a few minutes feeling in the moment.

- Allow yourself to feel relaxed yet alert.

- Your Calm Inner Peace is with you.

Try this for three minutes. When you finish stay still for a while and feel Calm Inner Peace.

Reflection Page (14) and Weekly Review

Date: Location:

Thinking about today and your previous sessions this week, reflect on your meditations.

Today's Session:

Weekly Review – Looking Back

- Summarise your overall experience of your meditations:

- Describe any recurring challenges and how you approached them:

- Describe how your meditations have helped you:

- What are you proud of this week? Allow yourself to celebrate successes and achievements:

Companion Message:

Brilliant! You have now completed a further seven days of meditation. This is all helping you move forward with your meditation practice. It is becoming more of a regular habit in your life. Your reflections are helping you and your sense of calm inner peace is growing each time you meditate.

Chapter 7: Moving Forward

This part of the Journal is all about you moving forward and having choice in the meditation practice you would like to use going forward.

Take some time to now select a meditation or maybe two or three that you felt comfortable using. To help you here is a reminder of the meditations covered in Part 2, Your Journal:

Meditation	Page
Pure Calm Meditation	40
Belly Breath Meditation	51
Breath in Numbers Meditation	54
Loving Kindness Meditation (Self)	56
Defrost Meditation	58
Loving Kindness Meditation (Others)	60
Nature Meditation	63
In The Moment Meditation	65

The Journal now has fourteen reflection pages that you can use to build your meditation practice. There is also a weekly review within the seventh and fourteenth session.

Allow yourself each day to choose and work with a meditation and then reflect on the experience.

Reflection Page (15)

Date: Location:

Guidance: Use short sentences or two or three words for each item. This will help you focus on the items that stand out. Keep it simple.

From this Meditation:

- Describe how you felt during and after this session:

- Describe any challenges you experienced during the session (thoughts, emotions, physical sensations):

- As a result of this session describe any benefits you can see from this session:

Reflection Page (16)

Date: Location:

Guidance: Use short sentences or two or three words for each item. This will help you focus on the items that stand out. Keep it simple.

From this Meditation:

- Describe how you felt during and after this session:

- Describe any challenges you experienced during the session (thoughts, emotions, physical sensations):

- As a result of this session describe any benefits you can see from this session:

Reflection Page (17)

Date: Location:

Guidance: Use short sentences or two or three words for each item. This will help you focus on the items that stand out. Keep it simple.

From this Meditation:

- Describe how you felt during and after this session:

- Describe any challenges you experienced during the session (thoughts, emotions, physical sensations):

- As a result of this session describe any benefits you can see from this session:

Reflection Page (18)

Date: Location:

Guidance: Use short sentences or two or three words for each item. This will help you focus on the items that stand out. Keep it simple.

From this Meditation:

- Describe how you felt during and after this session:

- Describe any challenges you experienced during the session (thoughts, emotions, physical sensations):

- As a result of this session describe any benefits you can see from this session:

Reflection Page (19)

Date: Location:

Guidance: Use short sentences or two or three words for each item. This will help you focus on the items that stand out. Keep it simple.

From this Meditation:

- Describe how you felt during and after this session:

- Describe any challenges you experienced during the session (thoughts, emotions, physical sensations):

- As a result of this session describe any benefits you can see from this session:

Reflection Page (20)

Date: Location:

Guidance: Use short sentences or two or three words for each item. This will help you focus on the items that stand out. Keep it simple.

From this Meditation:

- Describe how you felt during and after this session:

- Describe any challenges you experienced during the session (thoughts, emotions, physical sensations):

- As a result of this session describe any benefits you can see from this session:

Reflection Page (21) and Weekly Review

Date: Location:

Thinking about today and your previous sessions this week, reflect on your meditations.

Today's Session:

Weekly Review – Looking Back

- Summarise your overall experience of your meditations:

- Describe any recurring challenges and how you approached them:

- Describe how your meditations have helped you:

- What are you proud of this week? Allow yourself to celebrate successes and achievements:

Reflection Page (22)

Date: Location:

Guidance: Use short sentences or two or three words for each item. This will help you focus on the items that stand out. Keep it simple.

From this Meditation:

- Describe how you felt during and after this session:

- Describe any challenges you experienced during the session (thoughts, emotions, physical sensations):

- As a result of this session describe any benefits you can see from this session:

Reflection Page (23)

Date: Location:

Guidance: Use short sentences or two or three words for each item. This will help you focus on the items that stand out. Keep it simple.

From this Meditation:

- Describe how you felt during and after this session:

- Describe any challenges you experienced during the session (thoughts, emotions, physical sensations):

- As a result of this session describe any benefits you can see from this session:

Reflection Page (24)

Date: Location:

Guidance: Use short sentences or two or three words for each item. This will help you focus on the items that stand out. Keep it simple.

From this Meditation:

- Describe how you felt during and after this session:

- Describe any challenges you experienced during the session (thoughts, emotions, physical sensations):

- As a result of this session describe any benefits you can see from this session:

Reflection Page (25)

Date: Location:

Guidance: Use short sentences or two or three words for each item. This will help you focus on the items that stand out. Keep it simple.

From this Meditation:

- Describe how you felt during and after this session:

- Describe any challenges you experienced during the session (thoughts, emotions, physical sensations):

- As a result of this session describe any benefits you can see from this session:

Reflection Page (26)

Date: Location:

Guidance: Use short sentences or two or three words for each item. This will help you focus on the items that stand out. Keep it simple.

From this Meditation:

- Describe how you felt during and after this session:

- Describe any challenges you experienced during the session (thoughts, emotions, physical sensations):

- As a result of this session describe any benefits you can see from this session:

Reflection Page (27)

Date: Location:

Guidance: Use short sentences or two or three words for each item. This will help you focus on the items that stand out. Keep it simple.

From this Meditation:

- Describe how you felt during and after this session:

- Describe any challenges you experienced during the session (thoughts, emotions, physical sensations):

- As a result of this session describe any benefits you can see from this session:

Reflection Page (28) and Weekly Review

Date: Location:

Thinking about today and your previous sessions this week, reflect on your meditations.

Today's Session:

Weekly Review – Looking Back

- Summarise your overall experience of your meditations:

- Describe any recurring challenges and how you approached them:

- Describe how your meditations have helped you:

- What are you proud of this week? Allow yourself to celebrate successes and achievements:

Companion Message:

You have achieved so much, well done! Your calm inner peace is helping you in many ways.

Allow yourself to reflect on all you have achieved this far. Your motivation and commitment have helped you. Let's keep this momentum and allow meditation to feel natural and an everyday part of your life.

Chapter 8: Your Meditation Journey

You have now completed at least twenty-eight sessions of meditation. These sessions can be seen as the start of your ongoing journey with meditation. By doing these sessions you will have:

- Found a safe location, your 'go to' place for meditation.

- Identified a posture that works for you.

- Developed your approach to a Calm Breath, Body, and Mind.

- Taken the time to build meditation as a habit into your day.

- Started to make choices in the type of meditation that works for you.

Your Journal reflections will provide you with evidence of your challenges and achievements. Remember, focus on the positives that have helped you and the experience of meditation.

Look back on your Journal and note the key areas of growth and learning. This will help you with your motivation and commitment.

This book has had a key focus of providing you with guidance and support to having a meditation practice that allows simple steps to help you move to calm inner peace.

The essence here is to keep your meditations simple and easy to access. To take away the pressure you may feel to achieve something. By allowing yourself to release expectations you are freeing yourself to be in the moment of each meditation.

Having taken these early steps with meditation you may wish to continue with the sessions that work for you. Allow this to be a natural part of your day. Where you find calm inner peace and can carry this feeling into your day.

At some point you may also feel ready to move on and explore other forms of meditation. This is your choice. Do not feel restricted. Meditation is something that is unique and personal.

Examples that you may wish to explore include:

- Guided Meditation
- Mindfulness Meditation
- Movement Meditation
- Loving Kindness Meditation
- Spiritual Meditation
- Mantra Meditation
- Transcendental Meditation

This list is not exhaustive and indicates some of the variety that exists. A key thing to note is that you have choice in the type of meditation you practice.

Whichever path you choose for your ongoing meditation practice remember:

- it is the journey and experience of meditation that brings calm inner peace.
- you are allowing meditation to be a natural part of your life.
- you are truly special.

From the author:

Feel proud of yourself. You have come so far. May meditation help you and bring loving kindness into your life and to your thoughts, words, and actions.

May you walk gently in the world and feel loved all the days of your life.

Wild Pebble

If you found Meditation for Beginners helpful, please place a review on Amazon.com. It always helps to have reviews and feedback on books - thank you.

Made in the USA
Columbia, SC
11 March 2024

32441084R00048